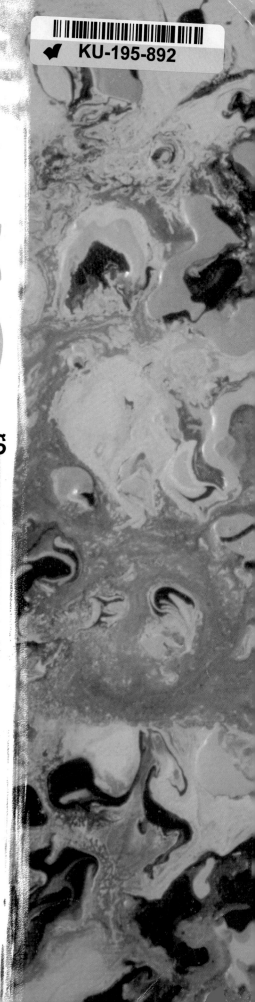

INTRODUCTION

Welcome to the fast and furious world of skateboarding.

No matter where in the world you find yourself, if you're the owner of a skateboard you can guarantee that you'll find a new group of friends in any city or town that you care to visit. Their world, and yours too if you're a skater, is one of ollies, grinds and switch hardflips. It's the world of skateboarding.

Skateboarding in the warm Californian night air.

Elvis is alive and well! He's doing rad 5.0 grinds on a mini-ramp.

Secrets, trick tips and urban legends are all waiting to be revealed. So get ready to find out more about one of the coolest activities around. Everyone's invited: tell your friends, and get on board.

Paul Heywood switch ollies over a hard landing place.

Skate talk starter kit

Set-up: If you're serious about joining the skate world you'll need one of these. It's your skateboard!

Rad: Short for 'radical.' Skate and surf slang for a good thing, i.e. 'that trick was rad' or 'you live in a rad pad.'

Nose: The front of a skateboard.

Tail: The back of a skateboard.

Ollie: This is the trick that'll have you pulling your hair out! It's the skateboard jump.

Fakie: This means travelling backwards, and not as you might think 'pretending to do a trick.'

Switch: Riding your board opposite-footed to the way that feels natural. Not to be mistaken for 'fakie.' As tricky as writing with your other hand.

Melon: Short for melonchollie grab, which is a jump where you grab the board with your leading hand behind the front heel. Also used to mean something you should protect with a helmet. . . your head!

5

History

Skateboarding began in the 1960s when a group of U.S. surfers got tired of having nothing to do when there was no surf and bolted rollerskate wheels to planks of wood. Little did they know that they had invented a pastime that would become as big as surfing! The blond, long-haired Californians called this new craze 'sidewalk surfing'.

FIVE CLASSIC VIDEOS

● *The Search for Animal Chin*
● Blind: *'Video Days'*
● H-Street: *'Shackle Me Not'*
● The *'Life'* video
● *Wheels On Fire*

Stacy Peralta

Stacy Peralta was a legendary Californian skateboarder who ploughed his winnings into setting up Powell Peralta skateboards. Powell Peralta helped sponsor amateurs and had a big skateboard team. The company is still a major force in the world of skateboarding.

Stacy Peralta carves a turn on a concrete bank.

Alan 'Ollie' Gelfand

Alan Gelfand, whose friends called him Ollie, invented the skateboard jump or grabless air, which was named the 'Ollie' after him.

The ollie is the basis for nearly every skateboard trick possible.

A fearless pool rider makes a cool carve.

This adaptable 1970s skater is using a huge pipe on the back of a lorry as a half-pipe.

Back in the early 1960s skateboards were just planks of wood with rollerskates nailed to them. As the years rolled on the humble skateboard went through a lot of changes. Among the strangest were clay (yes, clay) or metal wheels, as well as steel or plastic boards that came in all sorts of weird and wonderful shapes. Skateboarding became more popular and competitions were held to see who could master the sidewalk surfboard the best: slalom, high jump and long jump separated the best from the rest.

Equipment

The most essential part of any skater's kit is his or her trusty steed. Modern skateboards use precision parts. You can buy these complete, or in separate pieces so that you can build up your perfect custom skateboard.

If you're choosing your first skateboard you needn't go for the most expensive set-up in the shop. It's better to get a cheaper board to learn basic moves on. You can upgrade your components when you become more skilled. . . and more hooked! By then you'll know exactly what kind of set-up suits you best.

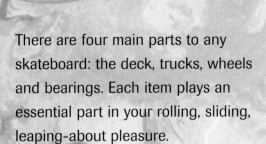

There are four main parts to any skateboard: the deck, trucks, wheels and bearings. Each item plays an essential part in your rolling, sliding, leaping-about pleasure.

Signature decks

Most professional skateboarders have their own 'signature' deck, which has their name and favourite design printed on it. Thousands are made and sold in shops around the world. The professionals get money for each signature deck sold.

Deck

A board made from seven sheets of Canadian maple wood glued together and pressed into shape. These 'decks' are shaped and usually printed with cool graphics.

Trucks

The trucks are the most technical part on a skateboard. They help you turn and carve and also grind obstacles. They come ready to roll, just adjust the tightness (tighter for harder-feeling turns, looser for easier turns) and off you go.

Griptape and bolts

Griptape is sticky-backed sandpaper that you apply to the top of the deck to help your feet grip the board. It's a particularly good thing when you're halfway down a handrail! Bolts hold your trucks to the deck: make sure they're really tight before you ride.

Wheels

Wheels come in different sizes and hardnesses. Larger wheels are faster, but smaller ones make it easier to flip the board. Softer wheels give a smoother ride; harder wheels help you snap the tail off the ground, making it easier to jump high.

Bearings

Bearings are there to make the wheels spin smooth and fast. There are loads of different types of bearing out there, but most will get you around very quickly.

9

Style

Every skater has their own skateboarding style and looks up to like-minded heroes within the skating scene. Some skaters won't stop practising until they're covered in bruises and have finally landed a spectacular, death-defying trick. Others are like neatly dressed technicians who spend all day perfecting complicated flip-to-grind tricks.

A perfect lump of marble gets a fast tech slide.

TRUE STYLE!

When you first step on a skateboard, get the basics together before you cover your deck with stickers and start washing your trainers before you leave the house. Cool-looking clothes or the very latest wheels may make you feel good, but true style comes from looking comfortable on your board.

The real point about skateboarding is that whatever you want to wear or do is up to you. Some people prefer to cruise the streets on longboards; others just want to get from place to place. No one style is best: skateboarding is for anyone who cares to step on to a board.

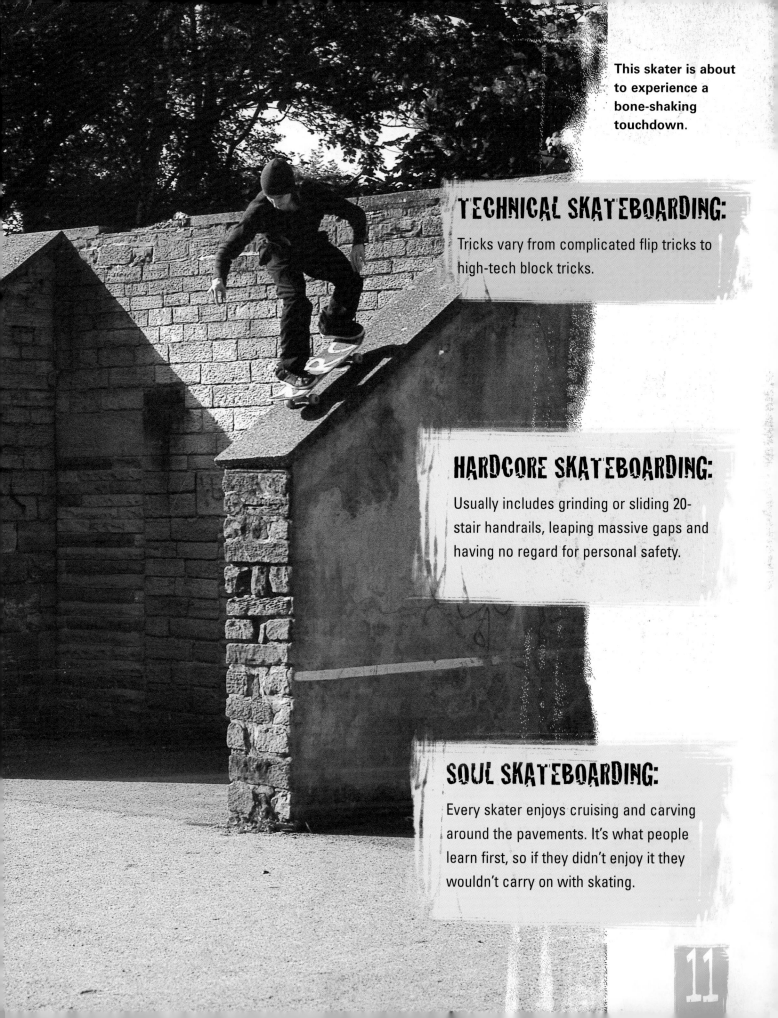

This skater is about to experience a bone-shaking touchdown.

TECHNICAL SKATEBOARDING:

Tricks vary from complicated flip tricks to high-tech block tricks.

HARDCORE SKATEBOARDING:

Usually includes grinding or sliding 20-stair handrails, leaping massive gaps and having no regard for personal safety.

SOUL SKATEBOARDING:

Every skater enjoys cruising and carving around the pavements. It's what people learn first, so if they didn't enjoy it they wouldn't carry on with skating.

BASICS

Skateboarding can seem quite daunting at first, but once you're rolling around the streets you'll be glad you put in the effort.

Three basic tricks are shown here. Be warned, all of them (especially the ollie, which is the first trick you need) take a lot of practice to get right.

trick tip: The Kickflip.

After you've hit the tail as in the ollie, slide your front foot up the griptape and off to the toe-side, causing the board to flip. Jump above the flip, then land back on the board's griptape side and ride off into the sunset.

trick tip: The Grind (5.0)

Roll next to the curb quite fast, then when you're ready pop an ollie and land on the curb. If you're going fast enough you should start to grind along the edge. After you've slowed down pop another ollie off the curb and ride away with a great big smile.

5.0 grind on the lip of an outdoor park.

12

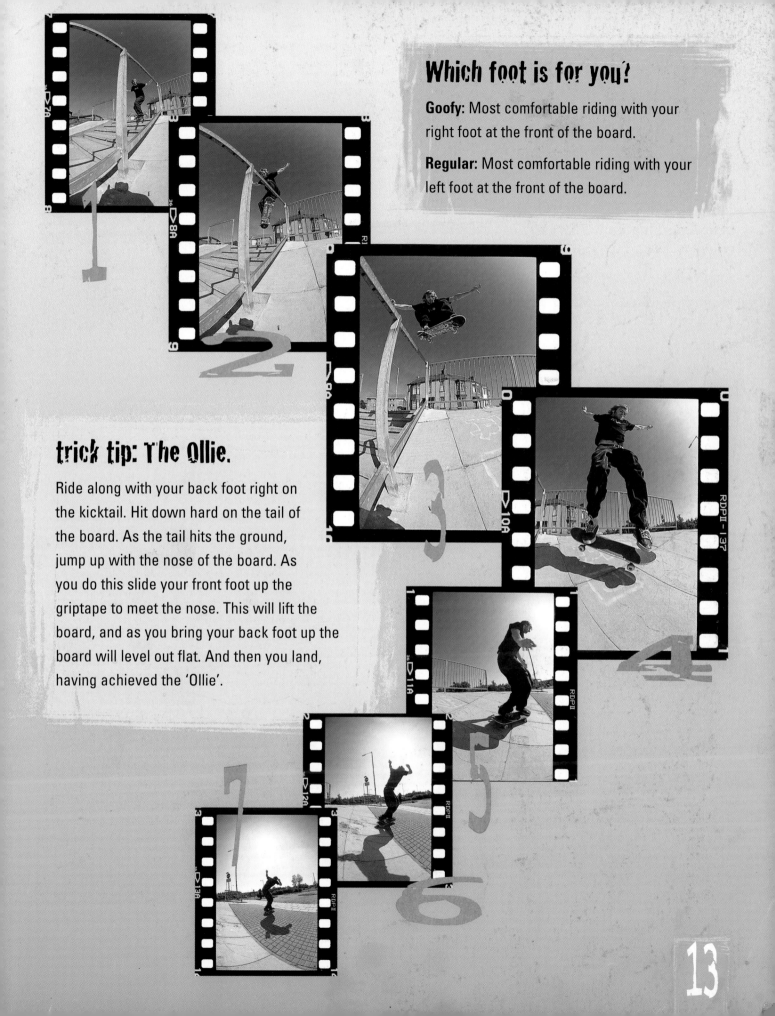

Which foot is for you?

Goofy: Most comfortable riding with your right foot at the front of the board.

Regular: Most comfortable riding with your left foot at the front of the board.

trick tip: The Ollie.

Ride along with your back foot right on the kicktail. Hit down hard on the tail of the board. As the tail hits the ground, jump up with the nose of the board. As you do this slide your front foot up the griptape to meet the nose. This will lift the board, and as you bring your back foot up the board will level out flat. And then you land, having achieved the 'Ollie'.

13

STREET SKATING

Street skateboarding is exactly what it says, skateboarding on the streets. The streets are where you live and work, and if you've got a skateboard they're also where you play! All you need for street skating is a board and some energy.

When you get into street skating, suddenly roads you have walked down a hundred times will start to look very different. Every obstacle – every curb, concrete block or rail – becomes a chance to do a trick. You and your friends will start to get to places by taking the route that has the best skateboarding opportunities, and life will never be the same again.

HANDRAILS:

When used by skateboarders these become sloped grind bars for sliding down. These days handrail stunts are a must for any skateboarder's bag of tricks.

SETS OF STAIRS:

Ollies and flips are the main tricks that happen down sets of stairs. Stairs vary in sets and sizes, so are good for learning tricks and building up confidence.

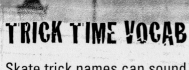

TRICK TIME VOCAB

Skate trick names can sound like a Martian's shopping list! Here are a few names explained:

Kickflip: This trick is where the board is kicked sideways and twists right round before the skater lands back on board.

360 flip: This is a kickflip as above, but as the board does its twist it also does a full turn underneath the skater. Looks very impressive to old people.

K-Grind: A stylish front-truck grind where the truck is angled while grinding. The K stands for Krooked.

Pop shove-it: The board pops up and shoves around 180 degrees without flipping.

50-50 grind: A basic grinding trick where both trucks are grinding (50-50 equals two trucks). A 5.0 grind is where the back truck grinds on its own in wheelie position.

Tailslide and noseslide: A balanced slide either on the front or back part of the deck.

BLOCKS & LEDGES:

Very popular obstacles, with skaters linking hard flip tricks with grinds and slides. Usually found in the city centres: a popular meeting place for skaters. Look for a tell-tale coating of wax (for sliding on) on your local blocks and ledges: you're bound to meet some skaters there.

Street Legend

FIVE MORE STREET LEGENDS:

Mark Gonzales

Jamie Thomas

Andrew Reynolds

Geoff Rowley

Chad Muska

Tom Penny, from Oxford, England, is one of only a few street skaters ever to master the hardest tricks. At the World Championships held at Radlands, England in 1994, Tom (who few people had even heard of at the time) landed every single trick he attempted.

Tom Penny performs an effortless kickflip.

Geoff Rowley seems to be solar-powered in this photo!

Penny travelled to the U.S.A. and set about becoming one of the most talked-about street skaters ever. He was seen across America doing tricks that had never been done there before. Video footage of Tom was incredibly rare, but more and more people wanted to see photos and videos of him. He had become an underground hero.

Chad Muska on the street course at a British contest.

Street skaters become legends by word of mouth, as people who have seen them skating tell their friends. Competitions can never take the place of a real street environment. Tom has now left the U.S.A. and is living in France, but every now and then photos of him skating appear, and the legend of Tom Penny is renewed.

WORLD-FAMOUS STREET SPOTS

Embarcadero (San Francisco, U.S.A.): Sadly now bulldozed, but lots of modern-day tricks were invented there. R.I.P.

Lyons (France): Brilliant street skating spots. Plenty of up-and-coming stars skating there every day.

Helsinki (Finland): Full of blocks, handrails and other skate architecture.

Hubba Hideout (San Francisco, U.S.A.): Famous ledge of angled concrete that often appears in skate adverts and videos.

South Bank (London, England): Often rumoured to be getting knocked down but always lives to tell the tale.

Stockwell (London, England): Fantastic concrete skate mecca: many skaters learn to ollie here.

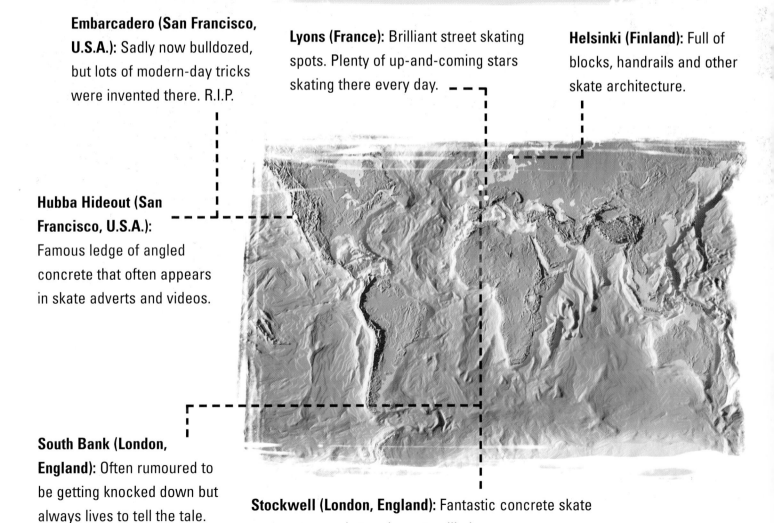

VERT SKATING

Vert skating has been around for a lot longer than street skating, and in fact was the most popular form during the early 1980s. Vert skating (short for vertical skateboarding) takes place on huge half-pipe ramps: skaters pull 6-foot airs and do crazy flip-grab tricks high above the actual ramp.

Vert skaters wear a selection of pads, as they sometimes fly nearly 20 feet above the ground with no safety net! Knee pads, elbow pads and a good, hard helmet are essential for ramp skaters.

CRAZY VERT GRAB NAMES

Roast Beef grab

Stalefish grab

Method grab

Melon grab

Sad grab

Vert skating can be great fun if you can master it with friends.

Luke McKirdy turns himself upside-down on the Birdhouse vert ramp.

18

VERT FACTS

● Legendary vert skateboarder Danny Way jumped out of a helicopter, landed on a specially designed ramp eight feet below, and rode it away smoothly!

● The typical size of a modern vert ramp is 11 ft high and 30 ft wide.

● In competitions, vert skaters get about 45 seconds to do as many tricks as they can. Whoever does the most tricks and stays on his board usually wins.

Bondi beach in Australia has a great mini-ramp: Vaughan Baker takes advantage.

Most of the tricks on a vert ramp happen above the lip (the top edge of the ramp). These are called air tricks and can range from an easy backside air to a mind-boggling trick variation such as a nollie heelflip grab revert! The lip of the ramp is used for grinding tricks as in street skating, but with a very high drop on one side to make things more interesting.

Tony Hawk: vert legend

Tony Hawk has been skating ramps for more than 15 years. He turned professional at the age of 14. Tony has invented many tricks, including the stalefish, the Madonna and the varial 540. He's also landed some tricks that no one else in the world ever has. In 1999 Tony landed the world's first 900, which is a spin of two-and-a-half turns.

When asked about his worst injuries, Mr Hawk surprisingly replied: 'Last year I broke my elbow. It's the first time I've ever broken a bone skateboarding.'

● Tony had a wooden full-pipe specially erected just so he could try and loop the loop, which he did with ease.

● Tony was also the first skater to land the elusive kickflip 540, which is a kickflip added to one-and-a-half full turns of the board.

Tony Hawk is without a doubt the most famous skateboarder alive: he's even got a computer game with his name on it. During his professional career he's won over 70 pro competitions and ten X-games gold medals. Although he's now over 30 years old, Tony continues to push the boundaries of vert skating.

Tony Hawk flying high in a competition.

Tony grabs his board
as he soars above the
Californian trees.

HAWK FACTS

● Very few people make a living from
skateboarding, but Tony has become a
millionaire.

● Tony Hawk wrote a computer program
which he sold for one million dollars!

● Tony was one of the original team
members of the 'Bones Brigade' a team of
top skaters that now has a legendary status.

● Tony's son Riley started skateboarding
before he could walk. Just imagine how
good he'll be when he's grown up. . .

SKATEPARKS

One of the best things about skateboarding is the fact that there are plenty of indoor and outdoor skateparks to visit. No matter where you live you are probably near a skatepark, which is a great place to meet other skaters. Most parks have a wide selection of obstacles, providing every kind of skateboarding all in one place.

INDOOR SKATEPARKS:

Indoor skateparks charge a small amount of money to skate all day long. They are usually made of wood and built by skateboarders. You'll find all the street furniture, from blocks and rails to artificial sets of stairs to leap down. If you fancy a quick ride on the vert ramp there will almost definitely be a huge ramp for you to practise your Tony Hawk moves on.

Indoor skateparks often have a skateshop where you can buy all the latest skate products, videos, etc. They will probably also hold local competitions where you can watch all the local stars, or even enter yourself.

Concrete bowls are great for ollies.

Funbox fun in among the skatepark crowds.

OUTDOOR SKATEPARKS:

Outdoor skateparks are constructed from concrete and resemble the surface of an alien planet. These parks are super smooth and great fun to cruise around all day long. You could find yourself carving down a huge 'snake run' or riding in and out of smooth 'moguls'. The best thing about these parks is that it's usually free to skate in them.

High above a South African funbox: ollie grab.

23

Safety

If you are jumping down stairs and sliding down handrails it's obvious that you're going to come into hard contact with the floor a few times when you fall off. This can be made less painful by knowing a few obvious tricks of the trade. Just make sure that when you are learning a new trick you stick by the rules and wear pads!

When you fall off the board it's better to roll out of the fall than to spread your arms and legs out to try and stop yourself. Scrunch up your body and roll sideways. Just roll away in the direction of the fall; you should be able to get up and jump back on board to try again.

Skate Protection

Wrist guards: Best for street skating, where you are more likely to put your hand down as you fall. They look like fingerless gloves, with plastic strips inside to protect your wrists.

Knee Pads: Mostly for ramp skating because when ramp skaters bail a trick they slide down the ramp on their knees.

Elbow pads: Elbows often get a bashing whether it be on the street or on the ramp, so they're useful for either.

Helmet: Protect your melon! Wearing a helmet is a must if you're flying around the rafters of your local skatepark. Vert skaters always wear a skid lid!

How not to do it: no helmet, no pads. Jumping down massive stairs could seriously damage your health.

SKATEBOARD DO'S

Do make sure that you wear pads while learning.

Do street skate with a bunch of friends.

Do check your board and make sure it's safe.

Do have a load of fun.

SKATEBOARD DON'TS

Don't attempt hard tricks too soon.

Don't cross other people's lines in skateparks.

Don't skate vert without friends.

Don't learn to skate without protection.

As well as pads, big, baggy hooded tops can protect your arms and denim jeans stop your legs being easily scraped. The most important safety advice is to use your brains: don't put yourself at risk by trying to progress too fast, or you'll probably find you can't skate for three months because you're in plaster.

COMPETITIONS AND SPONSORSHIP

Imagine getting loads of free products and cash for skateboarding! This is what happens to the top professional skateboarders. These skaters have put all their effort, time and energy into doing what they love. They started skateboarding because they enjoyed it so much, and ended up being rewarded with a dream lifestyle.

Jason Lee slides the handrail during a perfect comp run.

Competitions are held all around the world, and every year new kids turn up at these competitions to show what they can do. You can bet that these guys just skate for fun, too, but a lucky few will be seen by big skate companies and given the chance to earn a living doing what they love. . . skateboarding.

TOP FIVE WAYS TO GET SPONSORED

● Enter a competition and come first.

● Get some wicked photos in a skate magazine.

● Send a skate video of yourself to a big company.

● Join the competition circuit in your area.

● Steal Tony Hawk's book of skate secrets.

TOP FIVE COMPETITIONS

Radlands world championships.

Munster European championships.

X-Games skate championships.

Tampa pro and am competition.

Vancouver skate jam.

Technical tricks like these in a competition situation are a sign of real talent.

So, how can you become a professional skater? The best way is just to enjoy what you're doing. If you have fun you will skate well, then people will notice you and who knows? You could be the next Tony Hawk or Tom Penny.

Quiz

Balancing a tailslide on a vert ramp.

A DAY IN THE LIFE

Can you survive a day out skateboarding the streets?

8.30 a.m. You've just had breakfast and are ready to hit the streets. What do you need before you leave?
a) your set-up;
b) your krooked grind;
c) your stickers and clean trainers.

9.00 a.m. As you head towards the city centre you bump into another skater. He asks if you know who did a 'loop the loop' on a skateboard. Do you say?
a) 'Tony Hawk, of course.'
b) 'Umm. . . Evel Kneivel?'
c) 'Stacy Peralta, definitely. I think.'

11.23 a.m. You're skating some blocks in town and someone is grinding both their trucks on the ledge: what trick are they doing?
a) a 50-50 grind;
b) a rad switch fakie;
c) a kickflip.

12.00 p.m. Another skater starts to talk to you, and mentions someone jumped out of a helicopter on a skateboard. You interrupt him and say...
a) 'Yeah that was rad, it was Danny Way.'
b) 'That was me!'
c) 'Ooh! Ooh! I know who: it was Christian Slater!'

3.37 p.m. On the way home you try a new trick. You come off your board and hurt your knee and wrist. What should you have done?
a) worn some pads while you were still learning;
b) tried a lot harder;
c) four kickflips in a row.

11.31 p.m. As you fall asleep you start to dream about being sponsored. How did you make it big?
a) learnt to skate well, became confident and entered competitions;
b) wore skin-tight, day-glo shorts and a massive wig;
c) entered a competition as Tom Penny.

A beautiful sunset makes a great time to wind down: Ali Cairns spins a 540.

HOW DID YOU DO?

Mostly a) You're well on your way to becoming a serious contender for the golden skate cup. Keep up the good work and maybe you'll knock Hawk off the top slot!

Mostly b) You are a complete nutcase! Best stay in bed forever.

Mostly c) You spent most of your time looking at the pictures, didn't you? Go back, read the words, and expand your mind.

Glossary

Word:	Means:	Doesn't mean:
Air	A trick where you are in the 'air', whatever height you are off the floor	The stringy stuff on top of your head.
Am	A fledgling talented skateboarder.	Meat that is obtained from a pig.
Kicktail	The back end of your skateboard, the section you kick down on in order to perform an ollie.	A boot from behind.
Longboard	A longer-than-average board. Usually about five feet long (ideal for cruising).	An amount of very dull time when you have nothing to do.
Obstacle	Anything that you can skate, e.g. blocks, ledges, banks.	Fishing equipment belonging to a man called Ob.
RAD	A real good thing. Short for radical.	Abbreviation for 'Really Angry Dad.'
Revert	When as you're landing a trick you spin 180° at the last minute.	A sound that frogs make.
Snake run	A twisted, concrete downhill bowl.	A shout often heard in the jungle.
Spot	Anywhere that's recognized as good to skate.	What you don't like on the end of your nose.
Wax	Any form of wax, i.e. candle wax, beeswax. To make blocks and ledges grind easier.	The stuff in your ears. Yuk!

Books

Radical Sports: Skateboarding Andy Horsley (Heinemann Library). Includes information on competitions and clubs you can join.

Skateboarding (Activators collection) James Marsh (Hodder Children's Books). A more basic but fact-filled paperback with loads of great illustrations.

Dysfunctional Aaron Rose (Booth-Clibborn Editions). Cool photograph-based insight into the underground world of skateboarding.

Magazines

Sidewalk Surfer (Permanent Publishing). Andy Horsley works for Sidewalk, so they must be good.

Transworld Skateboarding (Transworld Magazine Corporation).

Slap Skateboard Magazine (High Speed Productions).

Web sites

www.skateboarding.com *Transworld Skateboarding* magazine's own skate site, filled with up-to-date info and ground-breaking tricks, interviews etc.

www.dansworld.com Dansworld skateboarding site. Up and running for a long time, this site has cool photos and interviews with all the latest skate stars.

www.exploratorium.edu/skateboarding/ Skateboarding Science: a good site to learn tricks and find out about skateboarding.

Index

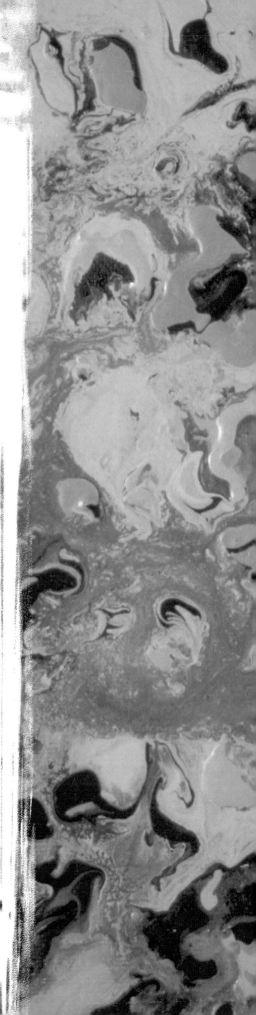

Picture Acknowledgements
The publisher would like to thank all those
who supplied photos for this book. All
photos Andy Horsley except: p.7 (top) Bruce
Hazleton; p.7 (bottom) Jim Cassimus; p.20,
p.21, back cover Wig Worland; sequence
p.24–25 Evan Bowman.